Thank you for choosing our "Sticker Boo
by Simple Kid Press!

WOULD YOU LIKE A
FREE
PRINTABLE GIFT?

SCAN ME

OR go to
http://bit.ly/simplekidpress

SIMPLE KID
PRESS

YOUR FEEDBACK MEANS
A LOT TO US!

Please let us know how we are doing
by leaving us a review on Amazon.

MW01132207

THIS BOOK BELONGS TO

_____

_____

TABLE OF CONTENTS

MY DINOSAUR STICKERS

MY DINOSAUR STICKERS

MY UNICORN STICKERS

MY UNICORN STICKERS

MY ANIMAL STICKERS

MY ANIMAL STICKERS

MY BIRD STICKERS

MY BIRD STICKERS

MY DOG STICKERS

MY DOG STICKERS

MY CAT STICKERS

MY CAT STICKERS

MY CAR STICKERS

MY CAR STICKERS

MY PRINCESS STICKERS

MY PRINCESS STICKERS

MY SUPERHERO STICKERS

MY SUPERHERO STICKERS

MY ROBOT STICKERS

MY ROBOT STICKERS

MY CHRISTMAS STICKERS

MY CHRISTMAS STICKERS

MY EASTER STICKERS

MY EASTER STICKERS

MY THANKSGIVING STICKERS

MY THANKS6IVIN6 STICKERS

MY HALLOWEEN STICKERS

MY HALLOWEEN STICKERS

MY SPACE STICKERS

MY SPACE STICKERS

MY MONSTER STICKERS

MY MONSTER STICKERS

MY FOOD STICKERS

MY FOOD STICKERS

MY INSECT STICKERS

MY INSECT STICKERS

MY SUMMER STICKERS

MY SUMMER STICKERS

MY WINTER STICKERS

MY WINTER STICKERS

MY SPRING STICKERS

MY SPRING STICKERS

MY AUTUMN STICKERS

MY AUTUMN STICKERS

MY BIRTHDAY STICKERS

MY BIRTHDAY STICKERS

MY CUTE STICKERS

MY CUTE STICKERS

MY AWESOME STICKERS

MY AWESOME STICKERS

MY SCARY STICKERS

MY SCARY STICKERS

MY BIG STICKERS

MY BIG STICKERS

MY TINY STICKERS

MY TINY STICKERS

MY U6LY STICKERS

MY U6LY STICKERS

MY _____ STICKERS

MY _____ STICKERS

MY _____ STICKERS

MY _____ STICKERS

MY _____ STICKERS

MY _____ STICKERS

MY _____ STICKERS

MY _____ STICKERS

MY _____ STICKERS

MY _____ STICKERS

Made in the USA
Las Vegas, NV
17 December 2024

14554098R00039